PERSONAL BEST

SOCCER

CLIVE GIFFORD

PowerKiDS press

New York

Published in 2009 by The Rosen Publishing Group Inc.
29 East 21st Street, New York, NY 10010

First Edition

Managing Editor: Rasha Elsaeed
Produced by Tall Tree Ltd
Editor: Jon Richards
Designer: Ben Ruocco
Photographer: Michael Wicks
Consultant: Steve Darlow

Library of Congress Cataloging-in-Publication Data

Gifford, Clive.
  Soccer / Clive Gifford. — 1st ed.
     p. cm. — (Personal best)
  Includes index.
  ISBN 978-1-4042-4441-2 (library binding)
  1. Soccer—Juvenile literature. I. Title.
  GV943.25.G548 2008
  796.334—dc22
                           2007042997

Picture credits
All photographs taken by Michael Wicks, except:
Cover Dreamstime.com/Dragan Trifunovic, 5 Magi Hardoun/epa/Corbis

Disclaimer
In the preparation of this book, care has been exercised with regard to advice,
activities and techniques. However, when the reader is learning or engaged in
a sport or utilizing a piece of equipment, the reader should get advice from an
expert and follow the manufacturer's instructions. The publisher cannot be, and
is not liable for, any loss or injury the reader may sustain.

Manufactured in China

CONTENTS

What is soccer?   4

The pitch and play   6

Training and clothing   8

Passing the ball   10

Receiving the ball   12

Movement in play   14

Attacking play   16

Shooting   18

Heading   20

Goalkeeping   22

Defending   24

Tackling   26

Set pieces   28

Glossary and Resources   30

Web Sites   31

Index   32

WHAT IS SOCCER?

Soccer, also known as association football, features two teams, each with 11 players. These players move a ball around a pitch using their feet, heads, chests, and legs—only the goalkeepers can use their hands and arms.

HOW LONG IS A MATCH?

A full game of soccer lasts 90 minutes. This is split into two equal halves, each lasting 45 minutes. In some competitions, such as the World Cup, periods of extra time are played if the scores are level after the full 90 minutes. Matches for younger players often last for shorter periods of time, and they may feature fewer players.

GOALS

A soccer team aims to keep possession of the ball and score goals, while stopping the other team from scoring goals. A goal is scored when the ball crosses the goal line between the goalposts and underneath the goal's crossbar. The team with the most goals at the end of the game wins.

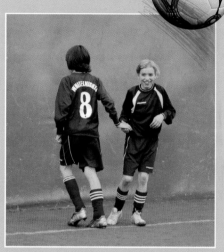

A substitution sees one player leave the field to be replaced by a new player. Coaches substitute players because of tiredness or injury, or when they want to bring on a different type of player. For example, they may wish to play an extra attacker and take off a defender.

crossbar   goalkeeper

goalpost

A goalkeeper gets ready to make a save from an attacking player. Goalkeepers are the only players allowed to handle the ball, and then, only when they are inside their own penalty areas (see pages 22–23).

Pitch positions

A team organizes itself with one goalkeeper and lines of defenders, midfielders, and attackers. The numbers of each type of player are used to describe the formation. For example, "4-4-2" means that there are four defenders, four midfielders, and two attackers. Coaches will choose different formations to suit the type of game they want to play. A defensive formation could have five defenders and only one attacker—"5-4-1."

goalkeeper

defenders

midfielders

attackers

The Manchester United and Portugal attacker, Cristiano Ronaldo, blasts a shot toward the goal.

THE PITCH AND PLAY

Soccer is played on a large grass or artificial pitch. The precise size of a pitch can vary, but the markings on every full pitch are the same. These include a large box known as the penalty area and a smaller box inside that, called the goal area. The four corners of a pitch are marked with corner flags.

The pitch

A soccer pitch is split into two halves by the halfway line, with a center spot and center circle in the middle. The game is started with a kickoff taken from the center spot, with all players in their own half of the pitch. A kickoff is also used to restart the game after a goal has been scored.

sideline

goal line

center spot

center circle

halfway line

goal area

penalty spot

penalty area

corner area

IN AND OUT OF PLAY

The whole ball has to cross a sideline or goal line for the ball to be out of play. If a ball goes out of play over a sideline, then a throw-in is awarded (see page 7). If a defender is the last player to touch the ball when it goes over the goal line, then a corner is awarded to the attacking team. The corner is taken from the small area beside the corner flag.

This player is running up the edge of the pitch with the ball under control. If she kicks the ball so that it curves out past the sideline in the air but lands inside the pitch, the ball has still gone out of play and a throw-in will be awarded (see page 7).

1 When the ball goes out over the sidelines, the officials will signal a throw-in. The player takes a throw-in from where the ball went out and must stand with both feet on or behind the sideline.

2 The player takes the ball back behind his or her head with both hands and then brings it forward, with both hands still on the ball. If he or she fails to do this or steps over the sideline, a foul throw is signaled and the other team is awarded the throw-in.

3 The player releases the ball with his or her hands following through toward the target. The player aims to get back onto the pitch as quickly as possible, and so get back into the game.

THE OFFICIALS

A soccer match is controlled by a referee and two assistants, both of whom run along the sidelines. These officials decide when the ball is in or out of play, whether a goal has been scored, and whether one of the game's laws has been broken. The referee uses a whistle to stop the game and has a variety of signals to show his decisions to the players and spectators.

When a player commits a bad foul, the referee can award a yellow card. A second yellow card in a game, or a red card for dangerous play, means the player must leave the field. His or her team then plays with one less player.

When the ball rolls over a defending team's goal line and the last player to touch it was an attacker, the referee and his assistants will signal for a goal kick. The goalkeeper or one of his teammates places the ball inside the goal area and kicks it into play.

7

TRAINING AND CLOTHING

Soccer is a very athletic sport and players need to be fit in order to compete successfully for an entire match. Training hard, warming up, and wearing the proper clothing will also give a player the best chance of success.

SOCCER BAG

A player's soccer bag is relatively straightforward, but there are important details worth paying attention to. The clothing you wear should be comfortable and not restrict your movement. Jewelry and watches must not be worn. You should also wear a tracksuit to keep you warm after a match or a training session.

Soccer jerseys are lightweight and should be a comfortable fit. They have either long sleeves (shown here) or short sleeves.

Tucking the jersey into your shorts is not just a matter of looking neat. It also gives a defender less chance to pull your jersey and hold you back.

Soccer shorts usually have an elastic waistband and a drawstring to keep them up.

Types of shoes
Soccer shoes come with different sole types for different conditions. Here is an astro shoe for playing on artificial pitches (top), a grass pitch shoe with wedges called blades to provide grip (middle), and finally, a shoe with round studs, which is also used on grass (bottom).

Long soccer socks are kept up using a sock garter, tape, or a piece of elastic.

Shin guards protect the bony front part of your lower leg from painful knocks.

Soccer shoes should fit your foot really well and offer support around your ankle. Good shoes are made of soft leather so that you can feel the ball during play.

The shin guards are held in place underneath the socks, usually by a couple of straps.

Whatever type of shoe you wear, make sure that the laces are tied securely and do not dangle to the ground where they could trip you.

WARMING UP

Before any training session or match, you should always warm up and stretch. Warming up can involve a mixture of jogging, skipping, and other exercises. These help to get blood flowing around your body freely to prepare you for the hard work ahead. After a warming-up period, you should stretch the key muscles in your upper and lower legs, your groin, and your back, shoulders, and arms. Stretches are performed gently and repeated, and help prevent injury. Ask your coach to show you how to perform a variety of stretches.

Stretching

These players are stretching the muscles at the backs of their legs. They are following instructions from their coach as they ease gently into the stretch and hold the position.

PRACTICE MAKES PERFECT

Training and practice are the keys to soccer success. Training will improve sharpness and reactions, and improve your passing, heading, shooting, and defending. It also gets you working with others as a team and improves your fitness, so that you can perform at your best throughout a long game.

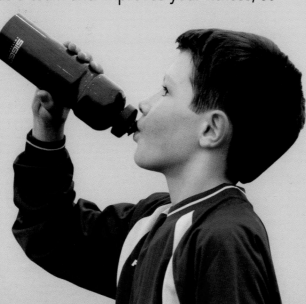

You will sweat a lot during a long training session or a full game of soccer. Players top up the fluids they have lost by taking small sips of water during breaks in training or at halftime.

These four players are involved in a "2 v 2" drill in a small area marked with cones. One pair of players tries to keep control of the ball and pass it to a teammate, while the opposing pair tries to intercept the ball. Training drills like these help to improve your game.

PASSING THE BALL

Passing moves the ball from one player to another, and good passing between teammates can get the ball into attacking positions quickly. Passing should be practiced as often as possible, and players should work very hard with their weaker feet so that they can pass using both their left and right feet.

TYPES OF PASSING

There are a number of ways the ball can be passed. Players can use their heads or chests to deflect balls to teammates. However, most passes are made using the feet and they can vary in their distance, height, and speed.

When making short, accurate passes, players tend to hit through the middle of the ball so that they keep it close to the ground. For more height on a pass, players lean back a little as they make the pass, and aim to hit through the lower part of the ball, lifting it off the ground.

These are the three main areas of the shoe that are used to make passes; the sidefoot, the instep, where the laces of the shoe are, and the outside of the foot.

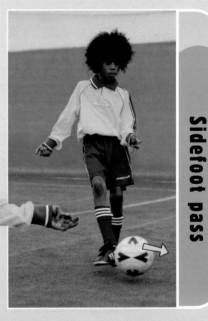

Sidefoot pass

1 The sidefoot, or push pass, is the most common pass in soccer and the most accurate over shorter distances. The passer places his nonkicking foot beside the ball and gets his body over the ball. His head is up and he is looking at his target as he takes his foot back.

2 The kicking foot is swung forward through the middle of the ball. The aim is to stroke the ball smoothly so that it skims along the surface of the grass to the receiver. The foot should follow through to point at the target.

1 The instep drive is used for long-distance passing because it can be made with much more force than the sidefoot pass. The player plants his nonkicking foot by the side of the ball and takes his kicking leg back.

2 With his arms out to help balance and his body over the ball, the player's kicking leg swings forward with the toes pointing down. The aim is for the instep to connect with the middle of the ball.

3 The kicking foot drives through the ball, with the ankle stretched down. The kicking foot follows through after the ball has left. Hitting the lower half of the ball with your body leaning slightly back will send the ball higher.

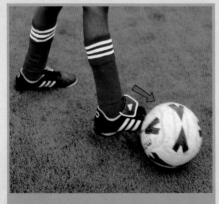

The outside shoe can be used to make a flicked pass. The shoe's toes swing outward and away from the player's body to nudge or flick the ball to the side. Aim to connect with the middle of the ball to keep it low. This type of pass can be used to send the ball "around the corner" for a nearby teammate to run onto.

FORCE, TIMING, AND ACCURACY

When making a pass, your thoughts should be on the teammate you are passing to, who is known as the receiver. Your pass should reach the receiver so that the ball is easy to control. A pass hit with too much or not enough force is unlikely to be successful. Timing and accuracy are vital, too. When your receiver is on the move, you have to time the exact moment you make a pass and aim it to travel to a point ahead of the receiver. That way, he or she will reach the ball and collect it without having to slow down or stop running.

Backheels

The backheel pass is used to pass the ball to a player behind and so reverse the direction of play. The passer swings his foot forward a short distance and then back toward the ball.

The player aims for the back of his heel to strike through the middle of the ball, to send the ball backward along the ground.

11

RECEIVING THE BALL

How the passer hits the ball is not the end of the passing story. If a well-hit and accurate pass is not controlled by the receiver, then the whole pass fails and the opposing team may get possession. Receiving the ball well calls for awareness of the game, an excellent first touch, and good cushioning skills.

CUSHIONING THE BALL

The ball will often travel toward a receiver at high speed. Cushioning is the skill of slowing down, or "killing," the ball's pace so that it is under control at the player's feet. It involves the player relaxing the part of the body about to hit the ball and moving this body part back as the ball connects with it. This helps to slow the ball down. The ball can be cushioned using your chest, thigh, or various parts of the foot.

chest cushion

1 This player watches the ball as she leans back to perform a chest cushion. She keeps her arms out with her hands open, so that her chest muscles are relaxed.

2 As the ball hits the player's chest, she relaxes and brings her arms and shoulders in to help slow the ball, so that it rolls off her and drops downward.

3 The ball drops to the player's feet ready for her to control and make her next move, such as a shot at the goal, a pass, or a run with the ball.

1 With her eye on the ball, this player bends her knee and raises her leg. Her arms are out a little to help with her balance.

2 She aims for the ball to land on the top of her thigh, which she relaxes and pulls back down to cushion the ball.

3 As the ball drops, so does her leg, so that both feet are on the floor ready to control the ball.

HIGH AND WIDE

Choosing which part of your body to control a ball with depends on the speed and angle at which the ball is arriving. Players learn to control the ball in many different ways. A dropping high ball, for instance, can be taken and controlled on the top of the thigh or on the chest. A wide ball may need the player to stretch his or her leg out to get it under control using the top or side of the shoe.

YOUR NEXT MOVE

As you are cushioning the ball, your thoughts should be on the next move. Receiving the ball well means you can get passing, shooting, or on the move and running with the ball as quickly as possible and so avoid being challenged by an opponent.

This player is using the inside of his foot to control the ball. He has turned his foot so that the inside is in line and faces the direction from where the ball is arriving. As the ball arrives, he brings his foot back to slow the ball down.

This player is cushioning the ball with the instep of the shoe. The foot is taken back and down as the ball arrives.

MOVEMENT IN PLAY

Moving with and without the ball is essential for a team to perform well in a soccer match. Players without the ball must know how to move into space to receive it. Players with the ball must be skilled at running with it, protecting it from opponents, and sometimes, they must be able to beat an opponent.

SHIELDING

When receiving the ball, you may not be able to move forward because an opponent is very close to you. In this situation, you may try to shield the ball by getting your body between the ball and the opponent. During shielding, a player has to look for his or her next move. This may be a layoff (a pass backward or to the side) or a sharp turn to beat the defender (see right).

OFF THE BALL

Moving into space often means getting free of a defender who is marking you (guarding you closely). A player trying to get free of a marker often uses a fake, or dummy, move, where he or she drops one shoulder and leans in that shoulder's direction, but sprints away in another. Quick changes of pace and direction are other ways of getting free of defenders and into a position to receive the ball.

The player in blue cuts away sharply from an opponent. She sprints into space with the aim of receiving a pass from a teammate.

Turning

1 The player in blue is shielding the ball. He turns and moves to get his body between the ball and the opponent.

2 The attacker makes his move, pushing the ball to one side and turning sharply as he protects the ball with his body.

3 Once the attacker has turned, he aims to sprint away quickly from the opponent.

BEATING OPPONENTS

In many situations, a series of quick passes helps to move the ball past opponents. Sometimes, though, a player may choose to go past an opponent on his or her own. This can be done by accelerating quickly or by dribbling. Dribbling is moving the ball forward with a series of close nudges and taps. It can be very useful for beating defenders, especially if it is combined with dummying (see right).

Dummying

1 A player dribbling the ball has already leaned to his left to suggest that he will be heading in that direction.

2 The defender is uncertain in which direction the dribbler intends to go and is flat-footed. The dribbler drives off his left foot to actually head to his right.

Dribbling

Good dribbling technique involves keeping your head up and looking around for your next move. The ball should never be too far in front of you and out of your control.

Push-and-go

1 This attacker (in blue) has spotted a lot of space behind a defender. The attacker decides to try a push-and-go move.

2 He sidefoot-passes the ball to one side of the defender carefully judging how much force to use.

3 He sprints quickly past his opponent on the other side to collect the ball behind the defender.

ATTACKING PLAY

Attacking is all about creating chances to score goals. When players receive the ball, they first look to get it away from their own penalty area, and then to attack and get inside or close to their opponents' penalty area.

DID YOU KNOW?

In 2001, Australia recorded the biggest win in international soccer by beating American Samoa 31–0.

Overlap

1 An overlap is where an attacker without the ball makes a run down the side of the pitch ahead of the player with the ball. The attacker on the far left makes his overlapping run so that he is not offside as the ball is played (see page 17).

2 The pass is played behind the defenders in yellow for the overlapping player to run onto. If successful, he is likely to be in a superb position to cross or shoot.

In this one-two move, or wall pass move, the player (right) makes a sidefoot pass to a teammate and then sprints forward. The teammate passes behind the defender so that the first player can run onto the ball, control it, and move forward or take a shot.

TEAM ATTACKS

Pieces of individual skill, such as successful dribbling, can sometimes create a goal-scoring chance. However, most chances are created by players working together as a team with quick passing and running to create space. Players can make runs that draw defenders to them, creating gaps for other teammates to move into.

1 A "through ball" is a pass made behind one or more defenders. The passer sees the run of his teammate and has to time and direct his pass perfectly to match his teammate's run.

2 The pass is threaded through a gap between the defenders. The receiver, timing her run so that she is not offside (see below), is now behind the defense with a clear run on goal.

Offside

Attackers have to be aware of the offside law—being caught offside will give the opposing team a free kick. A player is offside if, as the ball is played, he or she is closer to the other team's goal line than both the ball and the second-to-the-last opponent. A player is not offside if he or she is in their own half, receives the ball directly from a goal kick, corner, or throw-in, or is level with the second-to-the-last opponent. The player below is closer to the goal than the last defender as the ball is played. As a result, he is in an offside position.

OVERLOADS AND CROSSES

One key attacking tactic is to use the full width of the pitch to stretch the defense and obtain an overload—where there are more attackers than there are defenders. When the ball is in wide positions, it is often crossed. This is a pass made into the middle of the pitch, usually into the penalty area. Many crosses are hit high, aiming for the head of an attacker. However, when a team has made a fast break, a cross may be made along the ground for a teammate to run onto and shoot.

This player is crossing the ball into a crowded penalty area. She has to pick her target carefully. She aims her cross to beat the closest defenders and may target the front edge of the goal area. An alternative is to pull the ball back to a teammate in lots of space at the top of the penalty area.

SHOOTING

Attacking counts for nothing unless goals are scored. This most often involves players taking shots on goal. Shots can come from all kinds of distances and angles, but they must be accurate and on target to be successful.

SHOT TYPES

Attackers close to the goal may use a sidefoot pass as a shot to steer the ball away from the goalkeeper and defenders. From longer distances, attackers often shoot using the instep drive (see page 11), which generates a lot more power than the sidefoot shot. Some players can bend or swerve the ball on long-distance shots (see right). This can confuse a goalkeeper or take the ball out of his or her reach and into the goal.

Swerving the ball

To bend the ball to the left, use the inside of your right shoe to hit the right side of the ball and follow through straight.

To bend the ball to the right, kick through the left side of the ball with the outside of the right shoe. Follow through across your body.

This attacker in blue is about to shoot from close range. With the keeper in the middle of the goal, the attacker can choose to aim at either corner.

SHOOTING SKILLS

Quick decision making, placement, and good technique are all needed to turn shooting chances into goals. Opportunities come and go in an instant, and players need to stay alert if they want to fire off a good shot. Quick reactions can also see a player get to a loose ball first to take a shot.

You may find shots sailing high or wide, because you have stretched too far for the ball or do not have your body weight over it as you shoot. You should concentrate on making a clean contact through the middle of the ball and aim for a corner of the goal away from the goalkeeper.

Volleying

1 Volleying is striking the ball in midair. It can lead to a very powerful shot if it is played well. This player keeps his eye on the ball as it travels toward him. He plans to make a frontward volley.

2 He lifts his shooting leg at the knee and takes his foot back a short distance. He points his toes down and keeps his arms out to help him balance.

3 As the ball drops, the player swings his leg through, keeping his toes pointed toward the ground. He times his swing so that his shoe instep will meet the ball while the ball is still in the air.

4 The player's kicking leg follows through with a high knee lift. The player tries to keep his head over the ball as contact is made and the ball flies away. Leaning back is likely to result in the ball sailing off too high.

DID YOU KNOW?

Iran's Ali Daei has scored 109 goals in international matches, more than any other player.

FOLLOWING UP

Players should not relax and admire their shots. They must stay alert and follow up their attempts in case there is a deflection or block by a defender or keeper, or the ball hits the goal's crossbar or posts. Many goals are scored at the second attempt by alert attackers.

HEADING

Heading is a way of controlling the ball in the air. There are many different heading techniques that can be used for attacking, defending, and passing to a teammate.

HEADING TECHNIQUE

Many young players are scared of heading the ball, but heading does not hurt if you use the correct technique. This involves keeping your eyes on the ball until it hits your forehead—the ideal target area with which to head the ball. Start with gentle headers with your feet on the ground. Then you can build up power by arching your back a little and bringing your head forward to meet the ball, rather than just letting the ball hit your head.

Aim to connect using the center of your forehead. Although your eyes are likely to shut on impact, try to keep them open as long as possible to watch the ball onto your head.

This player has jumped to get above the ball, so that he can direct his attacking header downward into the goal.

1 The player on the right makes a cushioned header, relaxing his neck and taking his head back as the ball arrives. He makes sure that his head is above the ball so the ball is directed downward.

2 The cushioned header drops at the feet of a nearby teammate. Sometimes, a player can make a cushioned header to bring a high ball down to the ground for him to control himself.

HEADING VARIATIONS

In a match, different types of header are used in different situations. A gentle header aimed to the side may be used by a defender to put the ball out of play or by an attacker to nod the ball on to a teammate. Other headers are made with the player springing high in the air to get above an opponent or to get above the ball, so that he or she can direct it downward to a teammate or into the goal. Diving headers, when players throw themselves at the ball, are the most spectacular of all headers. They are used only as a last resort, when a player cannot reach the ball in any other way. Diving headers should be practiced using a crash mat on the ground so that you do not injure yourself.

This defender has made a strong defensive header. He has aimed to head powerfully through the lower half of the ball. This sends the ball up and forward, clearing it out of danger.

GLANCES AND FLICK-ONS

The glancing header is used to deflect the ball to the side, such as when an attacker is in line with one goalpost and wants to aim the ball for the other goalpost. Flick-on headers are often made with the top of the forehead, just brushing the ball to send it over a defender and on to a teammate.

As the ball is crossed in, this attacker has attempted a glancing header. He turns his head just before the ball arrives, and uses the center of his forehead to direct the ball toward the top corner of the goal.

GOALKEEPING

The primary role of a goalkeeper is to block shots on goal. However, good goalkeepers will also instruct defenders, command their penalty areas, stay aware, and position themselves to stop opposition attacks early.

Low save

ALERT AND AWARE

Goalkeepers have an excellent view of a game, but they may not have to save a shot for many minutes. Concentrating on the game is very important, since they may have to rush off the goal line suddenly to stop attacks or to receive back passes from teammates. If the ball is deliberately kicked back to them by a teammate, they cannot pick it up but instead must kick or head it clear. As an opposition attack develops, keepers should get into the basic goalkeeping stance with their legs shoulder-width apart, their arms in front, and body weight slightly forward.

1 This keeper is in a good stance, knees bent slightly, springy on his feet, and with his arms out. From this position he is able to move in any direction.

2 Moving from the ready position, the keeper bends the knee nearest to the direction he wants to dive, and begins to push his legs away to drop his body down.

3 The keeper lands on his side to block the ball. He can either catch hold of the ball, or push it away with his hands.

22

This keeper has dropped to the ground on one knee. His body is behind the ball as it comes racing across the ground. He gets his hands under the ball and scoops it up into his chest.

BODY AS A BARRIER

Goalkeepers put in hours of practice saving shots from all different heights and angles. The vast majority of saves do not require spectacular diving. Instead, they rely on confident handling and good footwork to get into line with the ball's path. This way, the keeper's body acts as an extra barrier behind his or her hands.

To take a high ball, maximize the advantage you have over other players by stretching your arms up and catching the ball at the top of your jump. Try to take the ball slightly in front of you, so that you can watch the ball into your hands.

Throwing the ball

When the keeper has safely caught the ball, he can restart the game quickly by throwing it to a teammate. Here, the keeper is using an underarm throw to roll the ball along the ground.

To get more distance on a throw, a keeper can use an overarm throw. This involves "bowling" the ball with a straight arm in order to get the maximum distance.

CATCH, PUNCH, OR DEFLECT

Catching the ball with both hands and gathering it into the body securely is the best option, but sometimes, the keeper is under pressure to reach the ball. If the keeper is uncertain about catching the ball securely, he or she may choose to punch the ball clear, or deflect it with an open palm around the post or over the crossbar.

Using both fists together, this goalkeeper punches through the middle of the ball to send it flying out of danger.

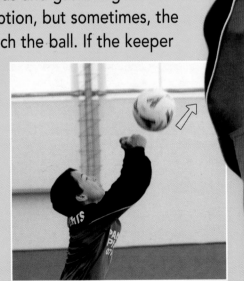

DEFENDING

A team without the ball has to defend and stop a goal from being scored. Good defending requires great concentration and awareness from all players in the side. It involves skills such as marking and jockeying.

MARKING

Marking is the guarding of either an opponent (one-on-one) or an area of the pitch (zonal marking). One-on-one marking calls on all your powers of concentration to watch the opponent you are standing close to. The aim of one-on-one marking is to prevent your opponent from getting into enough space to receive the ball. When you are marking, try to stay goalside (closer to your goal than your opponent) at all times.

WORKING TOGETHER

All players in a side defend when they do not have the ball. At the back, defenders mark the opposing team's main attackers and move with them as they make runs. At the front, strikers and other attacking players chase down opponents with the ball, trying to harass them into a mistake. Whatever position you play in, communicating with teammates is vital for a strong defense, as is getting back into a good position if an attacker gets past you.

As the player in yellow tries to control the ball, the defender in blue sprints to close him down. By getting close to his opponent, the defending player cuts down the attacker's options to pass and run.

Defenders from the team in yellow each mark an attacker as the team in blue plans to take a corner. The defenders stay goalside of the players they are marking and try to follow their movements.

JOCKEYING

Jockeying involves getting close to an attacker with the ball and moving with him or her, always staying goalside, to try and slow down an attack. The aim is to try to delay the attacker until another teammate arrives behind you. Then, you may be able to move in to make a tackle (see pages 26–27), or force the attacker away from the goal.

1 This defender in yellow has moved quickly to close down an attacker who has received the ball with his back to goal.

2 The defender gets up close behind the defender and tries to prevent him from turning without fouling him.

3 As the attacker moves, trying to find a way through, the defender also moves, taking the attacker away from the goal.

4 The delayed attacker has his foot on the ball to control it. However, the defender remains alert in case the attacker tries to perform a move to get past him.

TACKLING

When defending, there will be chances to try to regain the ball for your side by challenging an opponent for the ball. The most common technique used is the block tackle, which can be made frontward or from the side. Other techniques include sliding and poke tackles.

1 The defender in yellow races toward an opponent, who is dribbling with the ball. With the opponent not changing direction or passing, the defender decides to make a front block tackle.

2 As the defender gets close, he turns his tackling foot to present the whole inside of the foot toward the ball. He plants his nontackling foot and bends the knee to provide himself with a firm base.

TACKLING TIPS

Good tackling relies on you being strong, balanced, and decisive. Establishing a firm base with your supporting leg allows you to strike the ball with plenty of force, which will often wrestle it away from the control of your opponent. Timing your tackle is crucial. Lunge in too early or too late, and you risk an opponent getting away from you or you committing a foul. Remember, the aim of challenging is not only to remove the ball from an opponent, but also to get the ball under your team's control. If your tackle sends the ball loose, try to get it under control as quickly as possible.

Front block

3 Keeping his body weight over the ball, he strikes it through the center. The opponent loses control of the ball and the defender can take the ball away.

Side block tackle

The attacker in blue is running forward but is not protecting the ball, which is on the defender's side. The defender in yellow plants his nontackling leg and bends it at the knee. He hooks the inside of his other foot around the ball, dragging the ball away to safety.

Side tackle

1 The defender in yellow goes to make a sliding tackle from the side. He keeps his eyes on the ball as he bends his supporting leg—the leg closest to his opponent when standing side by side.

2 Getting as low as possible, the tackler reaches across the opponent and hooks his foot around the ball. He must make contact with the ball rather than his opponent, otherwise he will give away a foul.

POKES AND NUDGES

In some match situations, a full-blooded tackle may not be possible or even necessary. For example, when you are tracking an opponent running along the sideline with the ball, stay alert in case he or she loses control of the ball or pushes it too far ahead. This can sometimes give you the chance to race across and move away with the ball. If that is not possible, you may be able to poke or nudge the ball out of his or her path with the toe of your shoe.

3 The attacker loses possession of the ball. The tackler must get back onto his feet as quickly as possible to gain possession of the ball.

SET PIECES

When a soccer match is stopped by the referee's whistle or the ball goes out of play, it can be restarted in a number of ways. Kick-offs, goal kicks, and throw-ins are three types of restart. The other three main restarts—corners, free kicks, and penalties—are often known as set pieces.

CORNERS

A corner is awarded when a defender is the last player to touch the ball before it crosses the goal line. The corner is taken from the corner area closest to where the ball went out of play. Attacking players will crowd the goal area, expecting a cross to come in that they can head into the goal. Alternatively, the corner taker may play a short pass to a teammate who can cross from a different angle.

Corner taking

1 The corner taker can swing or bend the ball into or away from the goal. He may have made a signal to his teammates beforehand, so that they know where the ball is going.

2 Inside the penalty area, attackers and defenders will move, trying to get into a good position to either score a goal or clear the ball away from danger.

Free kick signals

Free kicks are awarded by a referee for a number of reasons, such as a player handling the ball or one player tripping an opponent. There are two types of free kick—direct and indirect. A direct free kick can be hit straight at the goal, but an indirect free kick has to be passed to a teammate first. The opposing team must retreat 10 yards (9 meters) from where the free kick is being taken.

A direct free kick signal

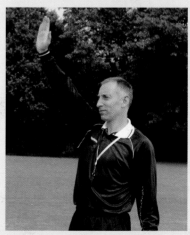

An indirect free kick signal

28

FREE KICKS IN ATTACK

When a team is awarded a free kick inside the opponent's half, its thought must be to attack—but this does not necessarily mean a direct strike on the goal. Free kicks from wide positions are often hit high into the penalty area. If a free kick is awarded in front of the goal and within range of a shot, then the defending side may line up a number of players to form a wall in front of the goal. The challenge for the free kick taker is to bend the ball around or over the wall, or to play a sideways pass to cut out the wall so that a teammate can shoot.

Free kick

1 This player in blue lines up an attacking free kick. The defensive wall protects one side of the goal with the goalkeeper protecting the other side.

2 The player decides to go for goal and to hit an inside foot swerve (see page 18). This will see him strike the right side of the ball with the inside of his right foot to bend the ball to the left.

3 As the player begins his follow through, the ball bends around the wall and toward the part of the goal not protected by the goalkeeper.

Penalty

1 This player has placed the ball on the penalty spot and completed her run up. She has decided to hit the ball using an instep drive.

2 She drives through the ball with her instep, looking to keep it on target. If the keeper does not guess and move the right way, then a goal is likely to be scored.

PENALTIES

A penalty is awarded for a serious foul or infringement that occurs inside the penalty area. The ball is placed on the penalty spot, and with only the goalkeeper to beat, it is a fantastic chance to score. Penalties can be hit hard or placed into the corners of the goal using the sidefoot.

GLOSSARY AND RESOURCES

Glossary

assistant referee An official who runs along the sideline and assists the referee during the game.

block tackle Challenging for the ball on the ground using the side of the foot.

cross A kick that sends the ball from the sideline to the center of the pitch, usually into the penalty area.

cushioning Relaxing and preparing a part of your body to receive and slow down the ball.

deflection When the path of a pass or shot is altered after it hits another player or a goalpost.

dribbling Moving the ball under close control with a series of short kicks or taps.

formation The way a team lines up on the field during a soccer match in terms of defenders, midfielders, and forward.

free kick A kick awarded by a referee to a team after a foul has been committed. Free kicks can be direct (straight at goal) or indirect (must be passed to a teammate first).

goal area Also known as the six-yard box, this is the small area around each goal, inside which a goal kick is taken.

handball Stopping or controlling the ball with the illegal use of the hand or arm.

instep drive A technique of making longer passes and shots by swinging through the ball and hitting it with the instep of the shoe.

jockeying Getting close to a player who has the ball and delaying his or her progress.

marking Moving with and guarding attackers to stop them from receiving the ball or from progressing in attack with the ball.

penalty area The large box surrounding each goal inside which a goalkeeper is allowed to handle a ball.

penalty kick A kick taken by a player from the penalty spot close to the goal and with only the goalkeeper to beat.

red card A player shown a red card by the referee is sent off and has to leave the pitch, leaving his or her team a player short for the rest of the game.

shielding When a player protects the ball by keeping his or her body between it and an opponent.

sidefoot pass A short, accurate method of passing using the inside of the foot.

through ball A pass sent to a teammate to get the ball behind defenders.

volley A ball kicked by a player when it has not yet bounced on the ground.

wall A line of defenders standing close together to protect their goal against a free kick.

yellow card Also known as a caution or booking, this sees the referee officially warn a player for a bad foul or other misconduct. Two yellow cards in a single game equal a red card (see above).

Diet and nutrition

Top international soccer players watch their diet extremely carefully and clubs often employ expert nutritionists to monitor players. Diet is also important at junior and amateur levels.

Eating a good, balanced meal several hours or more before a match gives your body time to get energy from the meal. A balanced diet contains a combination of the three main food groups—carbohydrates, proteins, and fats.

Complex carbohydrates are especially good for providing energy for performance. They are found in foods such as pasta, fruit, and vegetables. These foods are major features of a professional soccer player's diet.

Proteins are important in building muscle strength and stamina. Protein can be found in lean meat, such as chicken, and pulses, such as beans.

Books

Soccer Skills and Drills, Jim Lennox
(Human Kinetics Publishers, 2006)

Soccer Skills for Young Players, Ted Buxton
(Firefly Books, 2007)

Web Sites

Due to the changing nature of Internet links, PowerKids Press has developed an online list of Web Sites related to the subject of this book. This site is updated regularly. Please use this link to access this list:
www.powerkidslinks.com/best/soccer

INDEX

A

attacking play 16–17

B

backheel pass 11
back pass 2
beating opponents 15
block tackle 26, 27

C

chest cushion 12
concentration 22, 24
corners 6, 24, 28
crosses 17
cushioning 12–13, 21

D

defending 21, 24–25
diet 31
diving headers 21
dribbling 15, 16
dummying 14, 15

F

flicked pass 11
flick-on header 21
following up 19
formation 5
free kicks 28, 29

G

glancing header 21
goalkeeping 4, 22–23
goal kick 7

H

heading 20–21

I

instep drive 11, 18

J

jockeying 25

K

kickoff 6
kit 8

M

marking 14, 24
movement 14–15

O

offside law 17
out of play 6, 7
overlaps 16
overloads 17

P

passing 10–11, 12
penalties 29
pitch markings 6
pitch positions 5
push-and-go 15

R

receiving the ball . . . 12–13
red and yellow cards 7
referee 7

S

set pieces 28–29
shielding 14
shin guards 8, 9
shoes 8, 9
shooting 18–19
sidefoot pass 10, 18
slide tackle 27
stretching 9
swerving the ball 18

T

tackling 25, 26–27
thigh cushion 13
through ball 17
throwing the ball 23
throw-ins 6, 7
timing 11, 26
training 9
turning 14

V

volleying 19

W

wall pass move 16
warming up 9